You're My Best Friend, LORD

You're My Best Friend, Lord

LOIS WALFRID JOHNSON

Art by Judy Swanson

Augsburg Publishing House
Minneapolis, Minnesota

Dedicated to five nieces made beautiful
by God's love:

Laura, Luann, and Christine,
Kirsten and Karrin

CONTENTS

PREFACE

Do you ever feel like a sparrow fluffing its feathers in an icy wind? Or like a rocket ready to burst in a shower of red-hot sparks? Or maybe even like a bud opening to the sunlight of the fun of being alive?

After my first book, *Just a Minute, Lord,* was published, I received letters from many girls who knew all those feelings. Since then, I've had the chance to talk with many others —girls who told me about their good times, their bad times, their questions, and also their beliefs.

A few of these girls are members of the class I teach, and I would like to thank them for sharing their experiences with me. A number of the topics in this book grew out of the questions they asked. Some of the conversations are ones they have given me permission to pass on to you.

And so, as you turn these pages, I hope that you will realize there are other girls like you—others who have wondered and asked. You may want to use this book for your own devotions or for the times when questions pop into your head. Or you might like to talk with your friends to see which ideas mean something in your everyday lives.

My appreciation to those who have helped to shape this book—my neighbors, the Saturday Club, and those who supported me with prayer. Special thanks to my husband Roy for enriching my work by sharing his understanding of those whom he teaches.

My love to you as you read this book. I hope you'll discover that whoever you are, God's love can make you beautiful inside—that he will walk with you wherever you go.

I hope, too, you'll want to say, "You're my best friend, Lord."

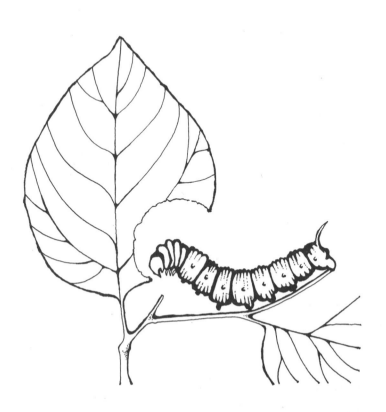

Squirm, Caterpillar, Squirm

"I'd give a lot to be just like Nancy. She's got it made."

We've all heard those words, haven't we? Maybe we've even said them. Or perhaps they sounded like this:

"Kim can play the piano. Debbie can do needlepoint, and Tammy always seems to have a smile for everyone.

"Then there's me."

Recognize the feeling?

It's like a squirming green caterpillar chewing away at our insides, isn't it?

And that's just what envy is—wanting what other people have, letting that want destroy something inside of us.

As the caterpillar of envy nibbles our insides we start feeling like a squashed tomato.

We think we're a total loss—not doing anything as well as other people do.

But wait! Let's think about it some more.

"I always used to compare my worst with everyone else's best," said one fourteen-year-old.

Ah ha! You too? No wonder it's hard to come up smiling.

Perhaps we're like the members of a seventh-grade class. They were asked to answer two questions: "What do most people think is the *best* thing about me?" and "What do most people think is the *worst* thing about me?"

No one had any problem naming the bad things. In fact, one girl asked, "Shall I make a list?"

Yet only a few could name the best things about themselves.

Being aware of what we do best is one of the most important things we can learn about ourselves. (And if you don't know, ask an adult who will tell you honestly.)

That adult might tell you about more than one thing you do well. You might be able to think of others.

Why not make a list?

Don't be afraid to write down good things about yourself. It's not a matter of being conceited. It's simply looking at yourself honestly.

Here's a possible beginning:

1. People think I'm thoughtful about how they feel.

2. I like animals.

3. I'm good at taking care of little kids.

4.

Any surprises? Perhaps you've discovered you do more things well than you realized.

Now, let's look at that list in two ways. First, we can decide whether we are underestimating our abilities. Too often we don't think well enough of ourselves. We forget that God created us with individual differences.

"Whenever my math teacher starts talking, I feel as though a cotton ball has replaced my brain," said Barbara.

Yet Barb has learned something important.

"Sure, I'm having a hard time in math," she admits. Yet she also says, "But I'm much better in English."

11

Many girls have abilities just opposite from hers. Their minds zip at lightning speed when facing math problems and yet struggle with writing a paragraph.

When we are trying our hardest and not succeeding, we can hug a thought to ourselves: "I'm not going to be jealous of my friend. There's something else I can do well."

On the other hand, envying another person can also be a reason for learning something new—even about being more beautiful. (More about that in another chapter.)

Rachel used to wallow in the mud of envy. Each time she thought, "I wish I could do that," she sank in further.

"Sometimes I *could* learn to do the thing I envied in someone else," she said. "For instance, that's why I can knit and play the guitar. But I couldn't succeed in everything.

"That's when I learned something else—to give compliments about the thing I envied in another person."

Some people are unwilling to tell others what is nice about them. It's almost as though they're afraid that they themselves won't seem as great.

But that's not the case.

Rachel feels sure enough of herself that she is able to reach out to others with a compliment.

"I took an honest look at myself," she said. "I know I'm not the most beautiful. I know I'm not the most talented. But I also know there *are* things I do well. And if I can make others happy by noticing special things about them, why not tell them?"

Why not?

Let everyone be sure that he is doing his very best, for then he will have the personal satisfaction of work well done, and won't need to compare himself with someone else.

Gal. 6:4 LB

Lord, help me remember the best thing about me so that I don't need to envy someone else.

Balloons Bobbing Before Me

She hadn't seen the elderly woman for several months. Now her words seemed to ring in Vicki's ears.

"My, but you've gotten big," she had said. "You must be the tallest one in your room!"

Tallest! Tallest! Tallest! Why remind me? thought Vicki bitterly.

If only she could scrunch herself into a tiny creature, she'd head for the nearest mousehole.

Sometimes when we feel different from others, we're able to do something about it. For instance, no one likes to be caught wearing a long skirt when everyone else is in jeans. Yet there are other things we must learn to live with.

During this time in our lives we might be growing faster than those around us. Take the boy living down the block. Even though he's our age, he hasn't even started to get his height. And it's hard to remember that boys often have their growth-spurt later than girls.

Or we may have the opposite problem.

"Shortstuff—that's me. I hate my nickname," said one seventh grader.

Instead of being too tall or too short we might feel we are too fat or too thin. We might have skin problems, braces on our teeth, or be developing later than other girls.

The list of all the things that we feel are wrong can be endless, can't it? And we haven't even touched on real handicaps such as blindness or deafness or the paralysis of an arm or leg.

Our problem may be something that someone else barely notices. Yet it seems big to us.

"When I keep looking at my bad points, that's all I see," said Jennifer. "It's like a giant balloon bobbing in front of me. Black letters printed on it say, THERE'S SOMETHING WRONG WITH YOU!"

Speaking of balloons, perhaps what we're concentrating on is something filled with air. What if we use a pin on whatever we feel is our weakness or handicap?

God accepts us as we are. Can't we accept ourselves the same way, saying, "Okay. There's the thing that bothers me. But what can I do in spite of it?"

What can I do in spite of it?

That's a big question, isn't it?

It isn't what we have or don't have that's important. It's how we feel about things. Sometimes a handicap forces us to accomplish a great deal more than we might do otherwise.

Before the days of Salk vaccine many people were left with paralysis after having polio. One of them is my friend Shirley Locker who lost the use of both legs and one arm.

Each time Shirley's hair needs shampooing, it takes her an hour and one-half to wash and set it. Before she leaves for work each morning she needs another hour and one-half to get dressed and eat breakfast.

Yet, though she must use a wheelchair, Shirley does her own cooking, washing, and ironing. She also types with her one good hand and has relearned shorthand so that she can take it with her left hand instead of her right. She teaches at a junior college, writes articles, and edits two newsletters.

Most important of all, she's fun to be with because she has something to say and is outgoing and friendly.

In spite of overwhelming odds, Shirley is living a useful, productive life. She is a person doing something *in spite of* her handicap.

In 2 Corinthians 12 Paul writes about this

when he says that he's glad to have something physically wrong with him. For it gave him the chance to learn how much God could help him. "When I am weak, then I am strong," he says.

In some cases our balloons will be with us all our lives. With other problems we'll find that as we grow older what seemed like a handicap will become something good.

Often the girl who thought herself too tall becomes the woman who is especially attractive because of the way she carries herself.

Recently I sat across a picnic table from a woman whose blue eyes sparkled as she talked. But soon I became aware of something else. I found myself listening, not only to what she said, but also to *how* she said it.

"You have a beautiful voice," I told her.

"Thank you," she answered. "I'm glad you like it."

Then she smiled. "When I was growing up, my voice was so low that I dreaded having a music teacher test me in front of the other kids. Every time I sang a note they laughed.

"Now people who hear me speak often tell me they like my voice. You can imagine how much it means to me!"

Another balloon? Sounds that way, doesn't it? And gradually the air went out of it!

God said, "I am with you; that is all you need. My power shows up best in weak people."

2 Cor. 12:9 LB

Thank you, God, that you will show me how to live with whatever balloons are bobbing in front of me.

Turning Mountains into Molehills

"I feel as though my life has been filled with firsts and unknowns," said Carolyn.

She named some of them. Starting junior high. Baby-sitting for the first time. Giving a speech.

Most of us know what Carolyn means when she talks about first days and unknown experiences. We also know the symptoms that can be a part of them — butterflies in the stomach, lumps in the throat, and clammy wet hands.

Sometimes it's a matter of common sense not to try something, especially if it's on a dare from others. We know we'll get hurt. But there's another kind of trying that we often face.

That's when we feel as if the Halloween

witch is waving her arms at us. "What's going to happen?" she asks in a crackly voice. "What if the other kids laugh at you?"

But there's someone else who had the same problem. One morning four-year-old Eric didn't want to dress for nursery school. Then he objected to getting into the car.

"I don't want to go," he stormed.

"Why?" asked his mother. "You've always liked it there."

"I'm not going anymore," he said, kicking a rear tire.

"But can't you give me a reason?"

"Because," Eric answered.

Finally his mother picked him up and set him in the car. For a month the same hassle developed whenever it was time for school.

"What's wrong?" asked his mother repeatedly. "Why won't you tell me?"

Then one day tears welled up into Eric's blue eyes. "Mommy—the teacher wants me to skip and I can't do it."

"To skip? No, I'm sure she doesn't think you should know that. You're too young."

But that night Eric held his mother's hand while the two of them skipped around and around the living room. At last the four-year-old managed to stay on one foot.

The next day his mother checked with the teacher.

"No, I don't expect anyone to know how to skip," she said. "I just wanted them to try."

Sometimes when we face difficult things that's all that is expected of us—that we should be willing to try.

To those of us who are older, Eric's fear of not knowing how to skip may sound a bit silly. Yet his problem involves something that starts when we are very young and might stay with us the rest of our lives.

"I want to do well," said Valerie. "But it makes me afraid to take on something in which I might not be good. What if I fall on my face in front of the other kids?"

"For a long time my fear of new things kept me from trying," Carolyn explained. "For me a bumpy little molehill in the grass was becoming a mountain."

Sometimes trying to avoid a problem can be the hardest solution. The mountain is still there to be conquered.

But what happens if we walk right up to it?

We can tell ourselves, "Okay, I don't know for sure if I'll make it. But I'm going to try—because I'll accomplish more if I try than if I don't do anything at all."

"What it really means is looking at my goal instead of my fear," says Denise. "When I'm giving a speech, it helps me to think about getting across whatever I'm saying instead of remembering my wobbly knees."

And perhaps there's something we're forgetting. As a member of God's family, we don't have to face anything alone.

Whenever we feel inadequate, we can tell our best Friend about it. With his help we'll do something far better than if we were trying it alone.

Like Carolyn, we might surprise even ourselves. "Another one of those firsts was trying out for junior high choir," she said. "But when I learned that God was with me I wasn't quite as scared. I thought sure my voice would croak. But guess what? My mountain became a molehill. I made the choir!"

> For I can do everything
> God asks me to with the
> help of Christ who gives me
> the strength and power.
>
> Phil. 4:13 LB

Lord, make me willing to try the things that will help me grow into a better person.

You Can Be Beautiful

"Hey, good lookin'!"

Emmy waved to the boy who had shouted from down the street.

There was a time she wouldn't have answered that call, supposing it was for someone else.

"I always remembered my big nose," she told me later. "Whenever I had a class with a boy that I liked, I rested one elbow on my desk. Then I cupped my hand around my nose."

She laughed. "I kept hoping that he wouldn't notice it."

Emmy was right. Her nose *was* too long, I realized. It was one of those things she had learned to live with.

Yet strangely enough I had never noticed her nose before. I wondered why.

When I asked her about it, she took me into her bedroom and pointed to a small sign taped to the bottom of her mirror:

NOT EVERYONE CAN BE PRETTY,
BUT EVERYONE CAN BE BEAUTIFUL.

How about that? Could we also count ourselves as beautiful?

"Not me!" you might be muttering, having only the image of a TV star in your mind.

Often we are made to feel that physical beauty is the most valuable thing we can have. Yet, although Christ was the most important person who ever lived, there is no description in the New Testament of how he looked.

We are drawn to Christ not by his physical appearance, but by what he was while he walked on earth. His love and kindness toward others made him a beautiful person.

Doesn't that mean that being beautiful is more than being pretty? It's a matter of putting together the right ingredients. And that's something all of us can do!

Let's take a moment to whip up a beauty malt, starting with the most basic ingredient of all—the ice cream. In other words, with the eyes, the nose, the mouth, the hair we were given.

When we stand in front of a mirror we can check them off one by one. But as we decide what we like about our faces (or what we don't like), we can do something more.

"Someone told me to say, 'Thanks, God, for the way you made me,'" said Kristi. "When I started doing that, I began to see all the good things about me."

Then she added, "Each day I ask myself, 'Am I doing my best with what I've been given?'

"If I fuss too much with how I look, it's as though I'm not satisfied with the way God created me," she explained. "But if I take too little time with my hair and clothes, it looks as if I've given up on the whole mess."

All of us feel better when we've just had a shower and washed our hair. Yet when we've done all we can toward personal neatness, there's something else that makes us beautiful.

By adding malt flavoring we develop an inner sparkle. Knowing that we are loved by God shows up in our faces. We have a special glow. A glow that makes us beautiful.

What's more, we have something to be happy about!

All of us know people who aren't fun to be around, simply because they're moody all the time.

"Grumpiness is a habit," says Judy. "And so is happiness."

A girl who wants to be beautiful can't afford to be moody. It takes real concentration to follow the advice of the commercial "Think happy today." To help us develop the habit of happiness we need balance in our lives—times alone as well as times with people.

"Sometimes I feel like a turtle pulling back into its shell," says Jackie. "I just want to go in my room and shut the door."

Now and then we crave a chance to be private. It's a good feeling to be by ourselves, isn't it? When we have a quiet time we can think about the ways our emotions and bodies are changing.

Or we can relive the special memories that make us warm inside. If we're discouraged, we can think of something we can look forward to.

After a time alone we're ready, like a turtle, to poke our head out of our shell again—to leave our rooms, ready once more to be with people.

As we know both aloneness and togetherness we are better able to keep the sparkle that makes our faces glow with loveliness.

But our beauty malt has another ingredient —milk that will smooth the problems out of our faces.

Isn't it easy to get bogged down with the things that bother us? And that shows up, marring the joy that makes us beautiful.

Twelve-year-old Kari realizes it doesn't have to be like that. She put it this way:

I really mean what I say, I believe in Jesus Christ. You need to believe in him or you have nothing. If you don't believe in him you have to worry all the time. But when you believe in Jesus Christ you don't have to worry. Any time you want to talk to someone he's there.

Being able to pray is like going to bed. We don't hold our muscles stiff all night, trying to float above the mattress. We sink down onto it and go to sleep.

When we give God our concerns, it's the same as dropping onto a mattress. We're able to rest because we know he's taking care of things.

In turn, he gives us an inner confidence that shines through as beauty. He helps us add the last ingredient to our malts.

Each of us responds in our own way, choosing chocolate, pineapple, strawberry, or whatever else we like. We're individuals!

But whatever way we choose to show it, that flavoring is an appreciation both of ourselves and of other people.

Part of being beautiful is to be thoughtful about our own personal value. Our bodies are something special—worth careful handling.

As we date, that careful handling may mean saying no. Yet one girl I know makes no apology for it.

"Being thoughtful means to give of my best, not of my worst," she says.

"I tell a boy, 'I think you're great. I don't want to do anything that would make you think less of me.'"

She has put all of the ingredients in the blender and the beauty malt she sips nourishes the specialness that is her.

She adds, "When I look into my mirror in the morning, I still want to be beautiful to *me*."

> Be beautiful inside, in your hearts, with the lasting charm of a gentle and quiet spirit which is so precious to God.
>
> 1 Peter 3:4 LB

Thanks, Lord, for making me the way I am. Help me to be a beautiful person.

Our Best Friend

Quietly Becca closed the back door. She paused for a moment, looking around the kitchen.

Voices from the living room. *Uh-oh! Grandma's here,* she thought. *I don't feel like seeing anyone right now—not even her. Maybe I can sneak down the hall to my room.*

Halfway there, a floorboard squeaked.

"Is that you, Becca?" her mother called. "Grandma would enjoy talking to you while I fix supper."

Inwardly Becca groaned. Now she was in for it. She paused, rubbed her eyes and cheeks, pulled her brush through her hair. Then she turned to the living room, determined not to show how upset she was.

But moments later it all spilled out.

"What's the matter, Becca?" grandma asked. "Usually you're full of smiles."

"Oh, grandma, you wouldn't believe what happened. Wendy's having a party Friday night. She invited everyone except me."

Becca sniffed, blew her nose. "All day long they were talking about how much fun it's going to be."

"Is Wendy someone you know well?" asked grandma.

"That's the worst part. She used to be my best friend!"

"That *is* awful, isn't it?" grandma agreed.

"I liked her," said Becca, her throat tightening again. "I told her everything. Now I hate her. I feel as if she kicked me in the stomach. What should I do?"

Grandma thought for a moment. "I guess there isn't too much you *can* do. Ask God to forgive you for the way you feel about her. And probably pretend that you don't mind hearing others talk about the party."

"Oh, grandma—are you kidding?"

"Don't you think it'll blow up like bubble gum if they know it bothers you?"

Becca was starting to feel better. "And pop in my face? Well—" she considered. "Maybe you're right," she added, a doubtful tone in her voice.

Grandma picked up the sweater she was knitting. "All of us want to be able to believe in people—but sometimes we can't They're human and they disappoint or hurt us."

"That's for sure," agreed Becca.

But that evening, as she closed the door of her bedroom, tears once again filled Becca's eyes, brimming over. Still thinking about the party, she turned out her light and pulled up the shade before sliding under the blankets.

A gentle breeze lifted the curtain and brought the fragrance of springtime through the half-open window. As Becca lay there, she could see the night sky, studded with stars.

Seconds later, a cloud blew across, masking the stars.

Then it passed. Once again Becca saw a clear sky. Stars brilliant. Light shining from a great distance.

In that instant, happiness welled up within her, pushing aside the aching hurt of the day.

The stars, she thought. *I'd forgotten, God. Always there, even in the daytime when I can't see them. A reminder that you're always with me.*

And tonight for awhile the clouds covered them. My hate for Wendy blocked out my view of you. But even so, you never left me. You're a friend I can count on.

For a moment Becca thought back to the discovery she had made some time before.

That God loves each one of us as individuals.

That he sent his Son to die on the cross so

that our sins won't stop that friendship from growing.

"Forgive me, Lord, for the way I hate Wendy for hurting me," Becca prayed. "Take away the cloud so I can see you again."

Then, as she looked up into the night sky, she remembered the one bright star with which God had told the whole world of his Son's coming.

"Thanks, Lord," she whispered. "I guess a friend isn't real unless he's with me like you—when I'm happy—but also when I feel bad."

Inside, the tight knot disappeared, and Becca felt her lips parting in a smile.

In her imagination the stars seemed to come nearer. So close she felt she could reach out and touch them.

Instead, she tucked one hand beneath her pillow. In a moment she was asleep, the smile still there after the tears on her cheek had dried.

> For God has said, "I will never, *never* fail you nor forsake you."
>
> Heb. 13:5 LB

When people disappoint or hurt me, remind me to look at you, Lord, instead of them.

If the Answer Is Love

Sally leaned around the doorway.

"Dad, I can't go to the movie, can I?"

Mr. Jacobsen looked over his evening paper. "What would you be seeing?"

Sally told him.

"No. I don't want you to go," he answered.

"That's good," said Sally, returning to the phone.

"What was that all about?" called Mr. Jacobsen as she finished talking and hung up.

Once again Sally stood in the doorway. "I really didn't want to go. I think the movie will be too scary. But it sounds better if I tell the kids that you said I couldn't go."

Sometimes our moms and dads can really help us, can't they? Often what they want for us is really what we want for ourselves. Like

Sally we find they can give us a good reason for saying no.

But then there are other times—the times when we really *want* to do something and our parents tell us no. Then our reaction isn't quite the same.

We feel like a bumblebee buzzing at a screen, trying to get out. "What's the matter with them?" we think angrily. "Can't they give me a chance to have fun?"

There are times when we long to grow up, thinking it will give us the freedom to do whatever we like. Yet maturity is not always something that develops with the years. It comes at whatever age we can handle responsibility.

Perhaps we can find better ways to handle that responsibility if we think about some of the reasons why our parents say no.

Melanie found one when she wanted to go to a party at Donna's house.

"Are her parents going to be home?" asked her father.

"Well—I *think* so."

"Better find out for sure," he told her. "Otherwise the answer is no."

"But why? I can take care of myself," said Melanie.

"Yes, most of the time," agreed her dad. "But if there are no adults in the house, other kids might push you into something you can't handle."

Another girl, Joan, discovered that safety is important to her parents.

"I'd like to go to the game Friday night," she said.

Her mother turned from taking a pan of cinnamon rolls from the oven. "Where is it?" she asked.

Joan named a nearby town. "I'm going with some older kids. Teresa will give me a ride."

"But she just got her license last week, didn't she? Is she used to driving on dark country roads?"

"Sure, mom. Quit worrying."

"But how can I help it?" answered Joan's mother. She set the pan down on a rack. "I'll probably never be able to forget something that happened to me a long time ago. One Friday afternoon when I was in tenth grade I overheard two girls talking as I left school.

" 'We're going to the game tonight,' said one. 'I just got my license and mom said I could have the car.'

" 'Well, drive carefully,' answered a teacher.

"But at two A.M. our phone rang. It rang a long time before my dad woke up enough to answer it. Because he was a pastor, someone wanted to know if he would go talk to two families. Four girls had gone in that car to the game. But coming home two out of the four were killed."

"Aw-w-w-w, mom. Why do you have to think of stories like that?"

Her mother found a plate and handed Joan a roll. "Look," she said. "I want you to have the fun of seeing the game. But I'd feel better if you took the school bus instead of riding with someone when I don't know if she's a good driver."

Sometimes we discover still another reason why our parents say no. They think we're too young.

That's a bitter pill to swallow. And perhaps the only cure is to wait until we are a bit older.

But maybe there is something our parents would be willing to substitute. So they don't think we're arguing, we can ask in a nice tone of voice, "Is there something else I can do instead?"

It might be possible to work out something that we'd like almost as much.

"It made me mad when my parents wouldn't let me go to something in seventh grade," said one fifteen-year-old girl. "It took me a long time to understand—and I wouldn't admit it to the kids for anything—but I guess I enjoy some things more because my mom and dad made me wait for them."

When we know why parents say no, it sometimes helps us understand why God wants us to obey them. Of course there are times when that seems very hard, for it doesn't change how much we want to do something. Yet God has promised happiness to those who do obey their parents.

And if we're lucky, we might see something more.

When Kris asked her father if she could do something, he put his arm around her shoulders and answered, "Sorry. I love you too much to say yes."

> We need have no fear of someone who loves us perfectly.
>
> 1 John 4:18 LB

Lord, when I'm upset because my parents say no, help me to understand how they feel.

Everybody's Doing It

"What's the matter with you? Everybody's doing it!"

Have you ever been the target of those words? And felt like a chocolate cake someone left on the ground?

It might seem that if you don't do what others say they'll stomp down on you. And one heavy footprint could turn something good into a glob of gooey frosting and squashed crumbs.

The phrase, "Everybody's doing it," often pokes its way into our choices when we are being tempted. Sooner or later all of us are going to be faced with doing something wrong. It's how we answer that temptation that counts.

Perhaps a tiny little corner of our mind whispers, "That really sounds like fun. I'd like to try that."

And we have to work very hard to let another corner of our mind do the speaking.

No matter what it involves, saying no is seldom easy. Especially if it's a friend doing the asking! The more we like a person, the harder it is to turn him down. We know we might have to stand alone.

When a social studies teacher asked his class a question, one boy gave an answer completely opposite from those given by the rest of the class.

The others booed. "You're wrong," they said.

But the boy defended his answer, giving the reasons for his choice.

The class fell silent, as one by one they realized he was right, even though he stood alone.

Today that boy is a man holding a responsible position in a large Eastern city.

For him and for us, standing alone is like paddling a canoe. We begin on one side of a lake. Our destination is a point on the other side. To reach it we pick out a tall pine tree and keep the bow pointed in that direction.

Now and then the waves become choppy. It seems rough going. Yet as we keep watching the tree, we get from where we are now to where we want to be.

When we are afraid to stand alone, we can

ask ourselves, "What do I want to be doing five years from now?"

And then, "Will the thing which is tempting me stop me from reaching that goal?"

Whatever temptation is involved—whether it's smoking, going too far with sex, or chemicals such as alcohol or drugs—keeping those questions in mind can help us avoid doing things which will hurt our future.

Handling temptations often involves the small, two-letter word *no*. Sometimes we cringe at using it. Yet learning how to say no is part of growing up, for adults also have the problem of turning down things people try to push them into.

"Others will have to respect my right *not to*," said Karen, her eyes sparkling.

As we say no to things that can hurt us, our courage builds up, shaping us into new persons.

Sometimes saying no means something more.

Through TV announcements and classes at school Lucy knew that smoking offers the threat of cancer. When her friends asked, "Want to go for a walk and a smoke?" she answered, "Well—I'll go with you. But I don't want a cigarette."

That was fine. The others said nothing.

Yet a week later one girl offered, "Here— want one of mine?"

Again Lucy said no.

But a month later she said yes.

We may have the kind of friends we need to get away from. Otherwise they'll keep us trying to straddle a rail fence. On one side lies a green pasture. On the other a rock-strewn field.

If we don't take ourselves away from temptation, there comes a time when we have to jump one way or another. Landing on the rocky side, we trip and fall.

Many adults who smoke wish they could break the habit. They agree on one thing— that it's better not to start.

With any temptation it's also easier to say no immediately. Then we get it over and done with instead of licking away at the temptation like a caramel sucker — seeing how good it tastes first.

As we face a temptation honestly, we can admit that we don't feel able to handle things by ourselves. We don't have to keep looking at whatever is wrong or at our fear of standing alone. Instead, we can remind ourselves that God has something better planned for us.

What's more, the Holy Spirit will give us the power we need to say no. All we have to do is ask for it.

Amy knew it wouldn't be easy when she told her classmates she didn't want to go along with what they were doing. One boy teased her, calling, "Hey, Amy! Are you chicken or something?"

Yet without closing her eyes, she prayed, "Lord, this is too big for me. Help!"

Then she tossed her head, forcing herself to laugh. "Yep," she shouted. "Cluck, cluck, cluck."

And her smile showed the world *she* was winning.

> Your strength must come from the Lord's mighty power within you.
>
> Eph. 6:10 LB

Thank you, Lord, that when I am tempted to do wrong, you will give me the power to say no.

Oops! I Goofed

"You should have seen how scared I was the first time I tried to jump a horse," said Paula. "And sure enough, when I went over the hurdle I fell off."

All of us know the sinking feeling that comes when we try hard but fail anyway. Take, for instance, if we're on a girl's softball team and strike out, losing the game, instead of hitting the winning run. Or if we come in just a few points too low for the grade we needed to pass a test.

When we goof with something we really wanted to do, we can't help but feel discouraged. Maybe our best just isn't good enough —or is it? What can we do about our failures?

We have two choices. We can hang our heads and say, "I goofed. I'm never going to try *that* again." Or we can take our mistakes and learn something from them.

It's no fun failing. But could it be that what seems like failure will someday turn into success?

Let's take a look.

The smell of burning cookies filled the kitchen. Mari snatched up a potholder, pulled open the oven door, and grabbed the pan.

But already it was too late. The charred mess was hopeless. Feeling disgusted with herself, Mari did the only thing she could— took the pan to the sink and sent her burnt offering down the disposal.

"Oh, wow," she thought. "What's mom going to say? I better make sure it doesn't happen again."

Sometimes our failure may be for a reason such as Mari's. Perhaps that's the first reminder that goofing will give us—to concentrate on what we are doing.

But there are other times when we concentrate very hard and give our entire effort. Even so, we just miss winning a blue ribbon at the county fair. And we are only a jack rabbit's whisker away from winning first place in the book-cover contest at school.

Yet, though we ache with wanting that prize, there are times when learning to lose is more important than winning. It may be that losing forces us to change our goals.

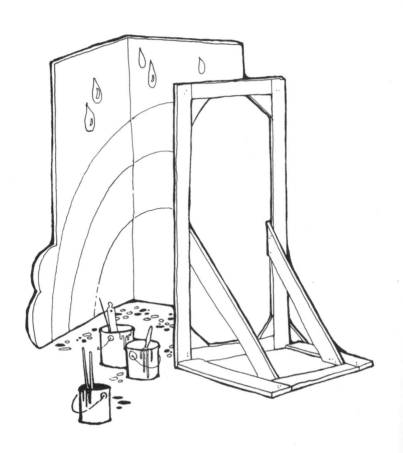

Brenda had worked hard to learn the school cheers. Her handsprings and somersaults were perfect, she thought. But when she failed to make the cheerleading squad, she decided she didn't want to sit around.

"I offered to paint props for the school play," she said. "At first I just filled in large spaces while an older boy did all the real work. But soon he started showing me how to plan things out."

Later on, Brenda decided she wanted to learn more about her new-found skill. Today she's a professional artist.

Failing might also give us the wish to work harder and accomplish something. One girl who nearly drowned on three different occasions pushed herself into becoming an excellent swimmer.

Another girl, Emily, envied one of her friends because she was able to make people laugh. "It was something I really wanted to do," she said. "Yet whenever I told a joke, I'd forget the punch line, and it would fall flat."

She was embarrassed when she learned she had flunked an English test. That same day a teacher told her to leave class because she was whispering and giggling too much.

"I sat in the principal's office thinking about where I was headed. I really wasn't succeeding at being the school clown. But I knew I could get good grades if I tried."

She got them. And because of her high average she won a scholarship which enabled her to go to college.

Heads or tails? Success or failure? And could our greatest success come when we are thankful about something else?

"I felt bad because I had goofed," said Jan. "But because of it I learned to depend on God's help."

Burned cookies? A lost game? An outer loss? Perhaps an inner gain.

And what happened to Paula after falling from her horse?

She got back on.

Two weeks later she was taking jumps like an expert.

> Always give thanks for everything to our God and Father in the name of our Lord Jesus Christ.
>
> Eph. 5:20 LB

Thank you, God, that even when I goof you can make something good out of it.

Doors in Our Walls

Patty yawned, fumbled for the lamp switch, and struggled to open her eyes.

The last thing she felt like doing was to get out of bed. *Why do some days have to be so hard?* she asked herself.

Theme due in English. Test in math. Report for science.

Yuk! It isn't worth getting up, she thought.

All of us have those kinds of days, don't we? Times when we wonder if we're going to pass a test. Times when our stomachs tighten from thinking about the work that is expected of us.

Now and then things seem too hard because we're a little short on sleep. Or people push us because they know we're able to do more than we're doing.

But for Patty there was another problem. She solved it by learning to ask herself a question: Am I doing my best at the right time, or am I waiting until the pressure is on?

Leaving things until the last minute causes tension we don't need to face. If we're already at that moment, it's too late for very much help. But before being pushed against a high stone wall, we might ask ourselves these questions:

Am I taking on too much?

In school we often don't have a choice about how much work we need to do. Unless a teacher gives the chance to earn a higher grade through extra work, we are required to do a certain amount.

Usually it's in things other than homework that the choices need to be made. And it's not that way only for us. You may have heard your mom or dad say, "Oh, I wish I hadn't taken that on!"

Erin has many talents and finds it especially hard to decide how much she can handle. She likes band and choir, competes in volleyball after school, helps with patrol, and takes part in Campfire Girls. For her it's possible to develop in many directions. Being in a number of activities is fun!

But even something that starts out to be fun drags us down if it's another leaf dropped on top of a pile that's too high. While it's not good to say no all the time, neither is it good to say yes all the time.

Sometimes we're able to find a balance by deciding, "Do I have some quiet spots in my life? Is this something that is really important to me?"

It might also help to ask, *Am I self-starter?*

Michelle waits until her mother reminds her before she does her homework. Sandra is just the opposite. More than likely she'll do well in whatever she goes into, for many responsible positions demand an inner drive.

"If I keep putting something off it seems like a bigger job than it really is," she says. "It's easier to do it on my own than to have someone nagging me."

She smiled. "I'm like most kids. I don't like to work. Yet if I didn't have to go to school I'd be bored with vacation." And isn't it hard to imagine *not* enjoying vacation?

Part of being a self-starter means to ask another question, *Do I begin with the hardest job?*

Often it helps to tackle the most disliked job first. Once we're tired it'll seem impossible to do.

"If I can do the hardest, then I sure can do the easiest!" says Kelli.

We might like to promise ourselves something nice at the end—dropping over to see a friend or doing something else we'd like.

We can also ask, ahead of time, *When is my deadline?*

One girl has learned to use a little "trick" on herself. "I plan to have something done before it's really due," Sonja remarks. "Then if I can't quite make *my* deadline I still have a little time left before the *real* deadline."

And last of all, let's decide, *Am I trying to be perfect, or am I trying to do my best?*

If we are trying to reach perfection, we don't give ourselves a chance to make a mistake now and then. With excellence we'll try to do well, but we are giving ourselves a door in the wall.

Carla puts it this way. "I know that I'm different from Jane and Carol and Mary Ann. Because something is easy for them, it doesn't mean I can do it perfectly." But she adds, "Just the same, I'm doing my best."

Perhaps in time we'll discover another secret. If we can answer these questions in the right way, we might find that we no longer feel as pushed.

"I even have extra minutes I didn't count on," says Patty.

> God has given each of us the ability to do certain things well.
>
> Rom. 12:6 LB

Guide me, Lord, in how I spend my time so that I can make the best use of my abilities.

Escape from the Mousetrap

Ginny felt the hotness creep up into her cheeks. She stared at her ring as she twisted it around and around.

Words seemed to fill the room, beating against her head.

"I have a daughter about your age," the store manager was saying. "Right now she needs a new winter coat. But if kids keep taking things from me I'm not going to have enough money to buy her that coat."

In surprise, Ginny looked up. She had never thought of it that way. Just as quickly she looked down again. She had been with other kids when it all started. Just for fun they wanted to see if they could get away with shoplifting.

"Have you ever taken anything before?" asked the manager.

Ginny nodded.

"What did you take?"

"Some little things. It just seemed like a joke," she mumbled.

"I know," said the manager. "That's what most of the kids tell me. They don't think about the fact that it's stealing. But I'm going to call your parents and have them come and get you. And I expect you to save your allowance and give it to me each week until the things you took are paid for.

"Does it still seem like a joke?" he asked.

"No." Ginny shook her head. "Today I came in because I really wanted something, and I didn't have enough money to pay for it."

"Very few of us can have everything we want," said the manager sternly. "And if I catch you wanting something again without paying for it, do you know what will happen?"

Ginny's fingers trembled. "The police station?" she asked, twisting her ring.

"The police station," he answered. "If you keep wanting things, your arrests will lead to a police record. And *that* will follow you the rest of your life."

Perhaps Ginny is like some of us. We don't always realize that something which seems small is actually very big. Not being able to control our wants can hurt us many years later.

It's really like riding a bicycle. A bike helps us get where we want to go much faster than if we walked.

In the same way our wants push us forward. If they are good ones, then it's okay. Some wants are worth going after.

But other times we hit a patch of sand and wipe out. We get hurt by being in too big a hurry for too much. We skid out of control, winding up with skinned knees and elbows.

More than likely there will always be someone having more than we have.

Adults often face this problem. They see someone with a bigger house, a more beautiful car, nicer clothes, more things. And sometimes grownups fall into a mousetrap, wanting the same kind of cheese their neighbors have.

If we want to escape the mousetrap, we need to begin right now, before it snaps down upon us.

It's a matter of deciding whether we will serve our wants, allowing them to control us. Or whether we will control our wants, making them serve us.

Sometimes wanting takes the form of a new game, special clothes, a tennis racket or skis. None of these are bad in themselves. It's the attitude we have toward them that counts. We might ask ourselves, "Why are they important to me? What is my goal in getting them?"

On an autumn day two junior-high boys were discussing the tennis shoes they had bought before returning to school. One had paid a great deal for his pair because he wanted a certain name brand.

"Mine are as good as yours," said the other boy. "What difference does it make to have that brand if another kind lasts just as long? Besides, my feet are growing so fast it's dumb to spend that much money."

The second boy had already learned how to make his parents' money stretch. Many girls do the same thing by sewing their own clothes.

Susan is one of these. She twirled, modeling a blouse she had just finished.

"I've always had to work for my money," she told me. "I save my allowance and earn extra by baby-sitting. Then I make a list deciding where I want to spend it."

Her friend Karrin had learned something else.

Her honey-colored hair swung about her shoulders as she grinned. "It's like picking petals from a daisy—you know, breaking them off and saying, 'He loves me—he loves me not.' But instead of that I decide, 'I want this — I can't afford that.' And it helps in keeping my money even with my wants."

Joshua said, "Choose this day whom you will serve . . . as for me and my house we will serve the Lord."

Joshua 24:15 RSV

Forgive me, Lord, for the times I've wanted more than is good for me. Help me to be in control of my money and my wants.

Walking a Tightrope

Georgia felt the frustration churning within her. In a moment she'd spit it out, like a pan boiling over on the stove.

"My little brother bugs me! My sister wants to do everything I do! And the kids at school are picking on me!"

Familiar problems? For most of us, yes.

There might be several reasons why it's hard to get along with others. Let's talk about some of them.

We might start by wondering, "Why does my little brother or sister wreck my things?"

It may be that they're too little to know better. But Kay caught on to something more.

"It's easy to say, 'I can't stand my little brother. Last night he put a frog in my bed.

This morning he ripped the stuffed cat I won at the fair.'

"It's much harder to remember the good times we had camping last summer."

Cindy, who has a little sister, noticed something else. "One day I saw her combing her hair the way I comb mine.

"A little while later I flopped down on my beanbag. My little sister didn't have a beanbag, but she sat down on the floor too—trying to lean back just the way I did."

Maybe the bugging and following around give us a clue to how much they really admire us. Of course, no younger brother or sister would admit that. Not for anything!

Yet Cindy found that if she put in a little bit of time, making the younger members of her family feel better, they would make *her* feel better by leaving her alone.

"Often I give them some of my things— things I'm getting too old for anyway," she said. "They really like that."

Sometimes, in addition to sharing, it helps to set boundaries. If we have a room of our own, we might talk to dad about getting a lock on the door.

If we share a room, it helps to have a shelf on which to put valued treasures. Mom and dad will probably be willing to tell a little sister that she can't touch anything on that shelf.

But now and then our trouble comes not because of our things being wrecked, but because others want their own way.

Sometimes it's a matter of being two jumps ahead of the problem.

Gail often baby-sits and knows that the three-year-old she cares for will turn cranky if she doesn't get him to bed on time.

"When I first stayed with him, he always answered, 'I won't do it!' to anything I'd suggest," she said.

"Now I've learned a few tricks to avoid power struggles. I get him started early enough so his worst side doesn't have time to come out."

She showed me the books she often takes along. "Instead of saying, 'Go to bed now,' I tell him, 'When you're in bed, I'll read a story.' And I make it interesting enough so it's something he looks forward to each time I come."

If we're the oldest and the sparks are flying with a younger brother or sister, it sometimes helps to consider the source.

"I get so mad that it's hard to take a cool look at things," said Anita. "Yet I know I'm the only one mature enough to do it."

"Often my little brother really wants an out —he knows he's wrong, but he has to fight to the end. The only way to stop it is if I can figure out a way to help him save face."

A different problem comes when we're in-

volved with someone our own age or older—
someone who puts us down every chance he
gets.

Tricia hurried down the street, pretending
she didn't hear the two boys talking.

All through autumn, no matter how high
the afternoon temperatures had climbed, she
had worn long-sleeved blouses because of their
remarks. Now a snowball splatted in her direction.

The shouting began again, "Hey, skinny
arms! Skinny arms, why don't you say hi?"

Sometimes a problem isn't really ours. It belongs to the person doing the teasing because
he or she is insecure—not sure of themselves.

In this case the boy doing the teasing had a
bigger problem.

"I know he's picking on me because others
pick on him — calling him 'Chunky' because
he's so fat," said Tricia. "He takes it out on me
'cause I'm smaller and younger and he can
find something to tease me about."

Yet though the problem really belongs to
someone else, it becomes ours because of the
way teasing hurts us.

Sometimes the only cure is to ignore taunts
until the person making them gives up trying
to bug us. Other times we can try to change
how we ourselves feel about the names they
call us.

"I thought about my nickname for a while

and realized it wasn't really so terrible," said one thirteen-year-old. "After that, it didn't bother me as much."

With some problems the solution involves something else—a compromise. Getting along with others can be like walking a tightrope. A highwire artist can't lean too far to the left. Nor can she lean too far to the right without tumbling off.

God doesn't expect us to make ourselves into a welcome mat, telling others to wipe their feet on us. Neither does he want us to give in and do something we know is wrong.

Yet we make a mistake if we feel that we must compete with everyone, always winning.

Each week the TV set crackled in protest as two sisters argued over which channel to watch. Each had a favorite show during the same time slot.

At last, tired of the hassle, one of them said, "Okay, I'll let you watch your show this week. But then you let me watch mine next week."

It takes a bigger person to put away defenses, backing down. Now and then we both can win by working out a way to do things together.

At other times the only way to stop fighting is to admit that we ourselves aren't perfect— that no one is right one hundred percent of the time.

"I guess the best way to get along with others is to get along with myself," said Marla. "And part of that is being willing to say, 'I'm sorry.'"

> And so I am giving a new commandment to you now — love each other just as much as I love you.
>
> John 13:34 LB

Thanks for loving me even during the times when I'm not so nice to love. Help me to love others the same way.

Kindling New Fires

They were munching popcorn at Pam's slumber party when her mother spoke up.

"I always looked forward to moving," she said. "It meant that I could keep all of my old friends but also gain a whole circle of new ones."

Pam's friend Lynn stared at her. Enjoy moving? She found it hard to believe. Yet she was to think of those words often.

Her days of living in a small Iowa town were numbered. On a morning less than a week away the moving van would pull up in front of her house. Before evening Lynn would be on her way to a large city.

Dread clutched at her throat each time she thought of it. "I don't want to leave my friends," she told herself.

She could still remember the shyness she had felt five years before when she sat at a fifth-grade desk, not knowing anyone in the room. No one spoke to her, and she was afraid to speak to them.

Yet, armed with the words spoken by Pam's mother, Lynn moved, and this time she found it easier. Whenever she felt a bit strange, she'd think, "I'm not losing all my old friends. I'm just gaining new ones."

Those are words we can take with us wherever we go. We might still be shy when meeting new people, but at least we'll make progress in getting over it.

Chances are each of us will move a number of times. If we melt like cheese on a pizza at the idea of meeting others, we can remember that shyness is a fear—a fear that gets worse when we think too much about ourselves.

Yet we can change that attitude. Let's try something.

How about being afraid of no one, yet respecting everyone?

Sometimes we forget that another person may be just as shy as we are. "Hi, I'm Mary Doe. What's your name?" is an opener which usually works.

Laurie is an outgoing girl who has many friends in her class.

One day a new girl at her school said to her, "I wish I knew as many people as you do."

Laurie grinned. "I have a secret weapon. I always try to ask people questions. I'm so busy thinking about what to ask that I don't have time to think about myself!"

We are all created as children of God and therefore each of us is deserving of his love. We don't need to be afraid of anyone, because every person on earth is equal—in God's sight.

But that also means we can't look down on anyone or treat anyone unfairly, for no matter who it is, God loves him as much as he loves us.

If we are treating someone in the right way, it'll be easy to act interested.

"I try to find out what others like to do," says Ruth. "If their interests are similar to mine, I soon feel as though I know them."

Acting interested might mean being willing to take part.

Whenever we join an activity — whether church, clubs, sports, or work projects — we have the opportunity to become better acquainted with others. Just like kindling a fire, we need to put wood and paper together to get things started.

Best of all, we don't have to worry about what we're going to say. Whatever we're involved in usually gives us plenty to talk about.

"Sure, I know it's a lot of work washing cars all day to raise money for our youth

71

group," said Kirsten, who was new to her church. "But it gives me a chance to talk to kids I didn't know before. And when I'm busy it's easier to just be myself."

She tossed her sponge into a pail and winked. "I don't even feel as if I moved here a month ago!"

> If I ride the morning winds to the farthest oceans, even there your hand will guide me, your strength will support me.

Psalm 139:9-10 LB

Thanks, Lord, that no matter where I am you will be with me. Help me forget my shyness by remembering to think about others.

Are You Part of a Group?

Trays thudded onto tables, silverware clattered. Voices filled the lunchroom, rising and falling in waves of sound.

Jody stood at the end of the cafeteria line, balancing her tray and facing the hubbub. Loneliness grabbed at her stomach as she wondered where to go. All around her small groups huddled. But where would she sit? None of her friends ate at the same time she did.

Most of us have faced a situation like Jody's when we felt stranded as though shipwrecked on a lonely island. We know the empty feeling of being left to ourselves when everyone else seems part of a happy little cluster.

It's a natural feeling to want to be part of a group. We're created in such a way that we need people.

Yet we'll find that the groups to which we belong mold us like a potter shaping clay on a whirling wheel. Some groups can hurt us; others can provide fun and make us strong.

How, then, can we become a part of the right group?

"By looking for friends in the right places," says Heidi.

She has good reason to know.

One Sunday morning she stood outside her church, laughing and talking with a number of her friends. Six-foot-tall Jim, who was new in town, noticed her and liked her friendliness.

That morning he found no chance to meet her. He decided to return, visiting a young adult meeting in the hope that she would belong to the group. When he discovered her there, he soon found an excuse to talk with her.

As he and Heidi became acquainted, they learned they had a number of interests in common. They also felt the same way about the things which are important.

That evening Jim offered her a ride home. Not too many months later he asked her to marry him.

As we meet people in different groups, we learn to size them up. We can ask ourselves, "What does the group stand for? Do they have the values which Christ has made important to me?"

If so, we can decide, "That's a group it would be fun to be a part of."

If not, we're free to think, "It doesn't really matter if I gain their approval or not."

When we feel uncomfortable with a group, it's often for a good reason. It's better to leave some groups than to stay just because we feel we have to belong to something.

We'll find that groups can offer surprises. Like a handful of agates, they might be shiny, smooth. They seem attractive, the best group to be in. Yet they may not be the people that offer the most to us later on.

Other groups are like geodes — ordinary, plain-looking rocks. Shaped like balls with rough, gray-white surfaces, there's nothing showy about the outside. Yet when someone cuts open a geode it becomes more than a round rock. Lining the hollow inside are beautiful crystals. Crystals just like the friendships which are possible with the right people.

When we wish to become part of a group like that we need to have the confidence to be ourselves.

"Easier said than done!" you might be thinking.

Right!

But there are certain telltale signs with which we might give away the fact that we're trying too hard.

What are some of them? One group shared some ideas.

"I always giggled too much," said one girl. "I really was trying to attract attention by being sure everyone knew I was having fun."

"I guess I bragged all the time," remarked another girl. "I thought they'd want me along if I made myself look good."

"What happened?" someone else asked.

"They didn't want me at all. They thought I was trying to be better than them."

A third girl spoke up. "I used to force myself on people. I just won't do it anymore. I want kids to like me because I'm me. When they do, they'll let me in."

Many of us find that the hardest part of being ourselves is to keep from freezing up when we feel out of things.

"I guess I always turned on a bored look—just for self-defense," said still another girl. "Or I didn't look at kids when they talked. That's what someone told me anyway. Then everyone thought I wasn't interested in being friends."

"That's kind of what I did," chimed in someone else. "And I always waited for someone to come to me. I didn't realize I was being selfish —that I should be reaching out to them."

As we reach out, trying to make others feel happy, our shyness will melt like a snowman in spring sunlight. If there's an opportunity to help someone, let's jump into it!

Often we can become a part of a group by being friends with one of its members as Lisa did. Soon after she moved into a new neighborhood, she saw a girl walking her cocker spaniel around the block. When school started a few mornings later, she learned that the girl's name was Beth and that they rode the same bus to school.

Yet each time Beth spoke to her, Lisa froze —wanting so much to be part of Beth's group that she couldn't think of anything to say.

Beth misunderstood, thinking Lisa didn't want to be friends. Each time they got on the bus, she went to the back with a group of girls. Lisa sat alone near the front.

Then one day Lisa was sitting on her front steps when Beth came by, walking her cocker. Just as they passed the house, the dog spied a squirrel on the edge of Lisa's lawn. Suddenly he bounded forward, straining at the leash. In that moment it snapped, and the dog tore ahead, chasing the squirrel up a nearby tree.

Beth ran after him, but as she tried to catch his collar the dog edged away.

With a bound Lisa jumped off the steps, moving quietly over behind the dog. Just before she reached him, he saw her and took off around the house.

"Sorry," she said to Beth. "Why don't you

go one way? I'll go another. Maybe we can corner him."

Each took off in a different direction. Finally they grabbed his collar, panting and laughing as they fell to the ground.

"Hey, thanks for helping," said Beth. "He's terrible if he gets loose."

She smiled shyly. "I thought you were stuck on yourself."

"But not any more?" asked Lisa.

Beth smiled again. "Not anymore."

> The Lord is my light and my salvation; whom shall I fear?
>
> Psalm 27:1 RSV

Thanks, Lord, for understanding my need for friends. Guide me so that I become part of the right groups.

Tumbleweed or Champion?

"I feel bugged all the time," complained Tracy.

"What's the matter?" asked her friend Jill.

"I want to be me. Do the things I want to do."

"Oh, sure. Me too," answered Jill. "I know what you mean. 'What time are you coming in? Where are you going? Who are you going with?' Questions like that."

"Just like that."

"I get the same ones," said Jill. "One night we hashed it all out."

"You and your mom and dad?"

Jill nodded. "They said they were bugging me because they really didn't feel they could trust me."

"Trust you?"

"Sure. They figured I didn't know how to take care of myself. They wondered if I could make good choices."

It's easy to feel that we're being bugged, isn't it? And it's hard to remember that many grown-ups feel as Jill's parents did.

They're asking themselves, "Can I trust her to make the right decisions, the right choices, when I'm not around to help?"

Trust is a funny thing. Like the ability of a championship figure skater, it takes a long time to be developed. Yet if we do the wrong things, it can also be quickly lost—like a tumbleweed blowing before the wind.

Most of us are made of championship stuff, aren't we? Not pushed away by the slightest breeze?

But how can we give our parents that feeling?

Lynnette realizes that her mom and dad like to know where she's going and when she'll be back. If they're home, she tells them before they have a chance to ask.

When they aren't around to get the message, she leaves a note on the kitchen table.

"Going to Jolene's," she writes. "I'll be back in time for supper."

Wanting to know that someone we love is safe is part of loving that person. And parents have been in the habit for a long time.

Parents also appreciate it if we are able to keep a promise.

"It seems as if I'm always late," moaned Dawn. "I really mean to get in on time, but I never make it."

You might already have noticed that it's always the same people who walk into church during the first hymn. Each Sunday they tiptoe down the aisle, trying to sneak quietly into the front pew—mom, dad, a boy with his shirt half tucked in, two girls with hair hastily brushed.

Having a sense of timing helps us whatever age we are. Sometimes it's hard to judge how long it's going to take us to get to a certain place. Yet if we give ourselves a little extra time for cushion we'll usually come out right.

Our parents also need to know if our plans change.

At the last moment Rhonda discovered that the party had been moved from Wanda's house to Bev's. Someone else gave her a ride there, and during the evening she forgot to call her dad to give him the new address where she should be picked up.

After forty-five minutes of waiting and circling the block where he thought the party was to be held, her father returned home. Feeling concerned and angry, he began calling other parents, asking, "Do you know where Rhonda and the others are?"

Another girl, Sarah, knows something else about giving her parents a feeling of trust.

"Hey, come on home with me," she says after school. "Bet my mom won't mind if we make a pan of brownies—that is, if we don't make too big a mess."

Sarah realizes her mother likes it when she invites friends over. Most moms do. It gives them a chance to see that we know how to pick our friends.

And it's another thing that makes them feel better about us.

So, what does being trusted really amount to?

Simply living up to the best that is within us.

Feeling a sense of responsibility toward everyone who loves us.

Realizing that we can't make exceptions of ourselves, thinking we can get by with something.

As one woman put it: "When I was growing up, my mom and dad trusted me so much that I wanted to live up to their belief in me."

And that brings us back to the problem of feeling bugged. We might still ask, "Will my parents stop bothering me if I do these things?"

Well, no one can guarantee what will happen with *every* mom and dad. But what can we lose? Chances are, if they know how thoughtful we are about the things they can see, they'll believe we can be trusted with more of the things they *can't* see!

And that will prove our ability to be champions, won't it?

> We confidently and joyfully
> look forward to actually be-
> coming all that God has had
> in mind for us to be.
>
> Rom. 5:2 LB

*Remind me, Lord, of my responsibility to those
who love me and most of all to you.*

Into New Life

Their newspaper was lying on the front step when the Williams family returned home from the weekend.

Julie picked it up, glancing at the headlines as she took it inside:

LOCAL GIRL KILLED
IN BOATING ACCIDENT

Below the large type was a picture of a girl she knew well.

A tight feeling closed about Julie's stomach. Sitting down quickly, she read the article. Then, still unable to really grasp the news, she looked up.

"Oh, mom, she died," said Julie, her voice seeming to come from a distance. "I can't believe it. She died."

Her mother knelt, put her arms around her. "What happened?"

"Here, read," answered Julie, still dazed. She pushed the paper into her mother's hands. "She was swimming in front of their cabin and a speedboat came too close and killed her."

Sooner or later all of us face the reality of death. Sometimes that reality comes because a pet that we love dies suddenly. Or perhaps a grandparent, a mother or father, brother or sister, or a close friend.

Whoever and whatever is involved, death usually forces us to ask questions. They may be, "Does my pet go to heaven? What is it like to die?" Or "What is heaven like?"

It helps to know all we can about heaven. Christ said, "I go to prepare a place for you . . . that where I am you may be also" (John 14:2-3 RSV).

As a result, we know that heaven is not a city full of strangers. Instead, it's a place where we'll find the best love possible, for our best Friend will be there to welcome us.

"Everything I've heard about heaven makes it sound as though we'll be happy there," said Karilee.

She's right.

Death is an experience in which God holds us by the hand, bringing us to a home where we will know joy. We don't know all of the details, such as whether our pets will be with us.

But we do know that everything necessary for our happiness will be there.

We might also wonder, "What happens to our bodies?"

In 1 Corinthians, chapter 15, Paul compares death to the planting of a seed. When we put a seed into the ground, it doesn't grow into a plant unless it "dies" first. The coating around the seed breaks apart in the same way as we unzip and take off our winter jackets.

Those of us who like to watch things grow know what happens next.

After rain and sunshine, we go outside and see the first green shoots breaking through the brown earth. Soon the tiny shoots unfurl their leaves and grow into delicious vegetables or colorful flowers.

Those plants are like our heavenly bodies will be—beautiful and full of strength. When people are sick or badly hurt, they shed weakness and pain through death, as if the seed coat were splitting apart.

Their new bodies are special ones. Paul says they will be full of strength and glory. What's more, those bodies will live forever.

Yet the most important thing to know about death is whether we ourselves are ready to die. As one person put it, "Only if we know how to live are we ready to die."

Part of knowing how to live is to answer two questions: "Do I believe that Jesus died to save me from my sins? Have I asked him to forgive my sins?"

For if we can say yes to those questions, we are ready for death in the same way that fourteen-year-old Becky Boyer was. Shortly before she drowned at a Minnesota Bible Camp she wrote this psalm-prayer telling about her personal faith in Christ:

Dear Lord—

How beautiful you are to me now! Your radiance fills my heart with joy and gladness. How wonderful it is to sit here and praise your name! I love to read your Word, I love to pray to you, but mostly I love you. My heart is singing alleluia because I know you. First you made me feel happy and joyous, then you helped me commit every part of me to you. You have also filled me with a beautiful power to witness to someone you love so dearly. I know how much you love me and I cannot express to any human person how I feel—only you can understand my joy because you have given it to me. I feel so happy that I'm just going to rest and think of heavenly things. I love you! I honestly love you.

For Becky dying was simply a matter of going to see a Friend whom she loved very much.

> Nothing can ever separate us from his love. Death can't, and life can't.
>
> Rom. 8:38 LB

Thank you, Lord, that you made it possible for me to believe in the Resurrection. Thank you for promising that your love will always be with me.

Hey, Big Hound Dog!

"Rrrrrr!" With an angry snarl the big dog jumped up on Liz, his paws pushing her backwards.

Frightened, she edged away, relieved when the owner grabbed his collar.

Most of us are like Liz — afraid of a dog whose temper pops out unexpectedly.

Will we be hurt? we wonder. We would just as soon keep our distance.

Instead, we'd rather play with a fun-loving puppy which has an even temper—a disposition we can trust—one who greets us with a welcome wag of the tail and likes to be petted.

Sometimes dogs have a right to be angry.

"Hey!" called Greta. From the hallway she'd heard their cocker spaniel growl.

Dashing into the kitchen, she picked up the

two-year-old visiting them. "No! No!" she said to the child. "You can't pull a dog's tail when he's eating."

In the same way we have a right, and even a responsibility, to be angry when we see wrong things being done. That was the mood Jesus had when he overthrew the tables of the moneychangers in the temple.

Lou put it this way: "It makes me mad when I see people polluting the environment."

"Or when someone big picks on someone little," chimed in Colleen.

But much of the time when our anger flares, it's not over things that need correction. More often it's a matter of seeing things out of proportion and letting them upset us.

Perhaps we've hurt people that way. Maybe they've drawn back, closing their feelings away from us because of something we've said.

"I often spout off with things I'm sorry for later," said one fourteen-year-old. "I'd like to be the kind of person others like. But what can I do about it?"

Most of us realize that it's easier to be thoughtful of others if we're able to get enough sleep. Yet right now we may be developing so fast that it's hard to get as much sleep as our bodies need. Sometimes our brains feel like eggs dropped on the floor. Our eyelids seem coated with sand from lack of sleep. Often it takes a real effort to get more.

In addition, we realize that our diets are important to us. Most of us want to eat fruits and vegetables because we care about our complexions. Yet following a balanced diet might have an extra bonus. Too much candy, or food containing a great deal of sugar, can make us feel irritable.

We can also try to avoid arguments when we feel especially irritable or out-of-sorts.

On days like that, some things may seem more of a problem to us than they would at other times of the month.

If we feel a bit edgy, we can try to think before we act or speak by asking, "Am I blowing this up? Or is it really important?"

Later we might discover that we're fighting over something that really doesn't mean that much to us.

Sometimes, too, we need to talk to someone before reaching the bursting point. We'll be less apt to explode if we tell someone our frustrations and worries before they build up too much. It's like opening a can of coke.

As we pull back the tab, the air comes out. We can handle things better because the pressure's off. The Coke goes into a glass instead of squirting us in the eye.

And will we still get irritable? Or be hounded by our tempers?

Of course. Whether we're 13 or 63. Even if we're trying hard, our angry words might still get away from us, like a dropped ball rolling down the street.

But that's where forgiveness comes in.

Now and then our school papers are smudged by cross-overs and sloppy handwriting. Think of those messy words as the times when we lose our tempers, as the moments when we're cross and irritable.

When we say, "I'm sorry," God reaches down with his giant eraser. He erases our sins so that we can start over with a clean sheet of paper.

And with that forgiveness we can once again be as happy as a friendly puppy—offering love to those around us.

> If you are angry, don't sin by nursing your grudge. Don't let the sun go down with you still angry — get over it quickly.
>
> Eph. 4:26 LB

God, forgive me for the times when I become irritable or lose my temper. Fill me with your happiness again.

Yay! Rah! Rah!

Kathy's face shone. Her quick smile lighted even the depths of her blue eyes. She was having fun!

All of us look forward to parties. Our enthusiasm bubbles up while they last. When they are over, we relive them with our friends, sometimes for many days.

As we go to parties or begin to date, most of us have only fun in mind—and that's great! This is a special time in our lives—and we need the excitement that being with others can bring.

Yet while we're having fun, we can also be learning about other people, and boys in particular. We can look for certain qualities, discovering what things we value most in the people we'd like to have for our best friends.

If there's a boy we especially like, we'll enjoy finding out more about him. We'll want to know if he builds people up or pushes them down.

"Most of the time I think he's great," said one high school sophomore, talking about a boy in her class. "Yet every once in awhile he starts throwing around sarcastic remarks. You know—things meant to be funny. But he goes too far and it hurts."

There's a fine line where sarcasm loses its humor and begins to bite. Usually we prefer being around someone who shows thoughtfulness.

Ken is that kind of person. One day as he pedalled down the street he noticed his five-year-old neighbor boy having trouble learning to ride his new bike.

"Hey, Marty! Want some help?" he asked.

Leaving his own ten-speed, he steadied the younger boy's bike until Marty felt able to take off on his own.

We might also think about how a boy looks at life.

One night, while driving Chrissy home, John's car coughed and suddenly lost power. Moments later he realized he was out of gas and tried to get the car to the side of the road.

"Uh oh—" he groaned. "I'm not going to be able to have you home on time. Your folks will be mad, won't they?"

Chrissy nodded, biting her lip.

"Come on, I don't want to leave you alone. We'll have to walk," he said, reaching across her to open the door. "And when we get to the gas station, I'll call your folks and explain that it was my fault. I should have been watching the gauge."

It takes courage to meet a hard situation head-on as John did. As time goes on he'll handle other things in much the same way.

For good or for bad, a person's future is shaped by the way he looks at things now.

As we get to know that special boy, we can also find out how he feels about Christ.

The spiritual side of a person's life shapes everything else he does. We enjoy having friends, and our friendships should include those who are not Christians so that we might share Christ with them. Yet it's important to choose our closest friends from among those who believe in Christ.

When Ginger started going out, she usually dated boys who did not attend church.

Often she told herself, "When it's time to settle down, I'll find someone who believes the way I do."

Years later she married one of the first boys she dated—a handsome man who had attended the same high school.

"Won't you go with me to church?" she asked him several times.

Finally he became angry. "Look. You knew what I was like when you married me. Why are you trying to reform me now?"

We can avoid this unhappiness if we choose our best friends and our dates from among Christians. In time that will help us, for the man we marry will be one of those whom we have dated.

"And I'm not leaving my husband up to chance," said Betsy. "I'm praying about it."

Yay! Rah! Rah! Can't we all?

As Christians we can begin now to ask, "Lord, guide my friendships with boys so that someday I'll marry your choice for me."

What will happen as a result? Our common sense will help us answer the questions we've listed. And God will help us see what's important about the boys with whom we become acquainted.

Let's keep our eyes wide open—ready for that sparkle of love which God can give them.

> Above all else, guard your affections. For they influence everything else in your life.
>
> Prov. 4:23 LB

Thank you, Lord, that you are going to guide me in my friendships. When it is time to marry, show me your choice for me.

When the Branch Splits

Nothing had gone right since Shelley had wakened that morning. And now *this*. She sat in a kitchen chair, a cold shiver running through her, even though the day was warm. She looked from her mom to her dad.

"You're really getting a divorce?" she asked. "But what about me? Will I live with you, mom? When will I see you, dad?"

Then she felt the tears pressing against her eyes. Jumping up, Shelley headed for her room, closing the door quickly before her parents could see her cry.

Sobs shook her body as she buried her head in the pillow. *Why? Why? Why?* she asked herself. *I should have guessed. They've acted strange for so long. They never seem to talk to each other.*

And then another thought struck her: *Do they love me anymore?*

Many of us have parents who are happy being together. But others of us may have Shelley's problem. If we are living with two people who are breaking up their marriage, it's natural to wonder how their decision will affect us.

We can remember that marriage and divorce are between two grownups. Something has changed the way they feel about each other. But that feeling is one kind of love. The affection they have for us as children is something entirely different.

"I learned that mom and dad still loved me very much," said one girl whose parents had been divorced. "That was something that stayed the same even when mom lived in one house and dad in another."

We may not ever know the real reason behind our parents' wish to live separate lives. Yet whatever it is, we can say to ourselves, "They love me now. They will keep on loving me no matter what happens."

If our parents are planning a divorce, there are some things which might help us face the problem.

We'll feel better if we realize how much our parents need us.

Mom and dad are also being hurt by what is happening. Some time ago they joined their lives together in marriage—a gift that God has given to man and woman. Now something has gone wrong.

A tight band around their hearts is squeezing the love they once had for each other. The fun they used to share is missing. Their lives are empty, and they need to hear us say, "I love you, mom. I love you, dad."

We might also discover that this is one of those times when we need to talk to someone about what's happening. Perhaps we feel we can talk to mom or dad. If not, sometimes a close friend can help.

Usually, though, it's better to find an adult who will understand how we feel. We might choose the mother of one of our friends, a favorite teacher at church or school, our pastor, or a school counselor.

We should feel free to say, "My mom and dad are getting a divorce. I'm upset about it."

And then, there's something else we can do.

It's normal to feel bad when we learn that something as important as our home lives is going to be different. We feel as though we've climbed a tree and the branch underneath us is splitting.

But that's where our best Friend comes in again. Our Friend who will help us no matter what is happening.

We can pray, "Lord, help me face whatever changes my life might bring."

Or we might still be able to do as one girl did.

Soon after her parents told her they were getting a divorce, she said to her father, "Dad, I'm sorry you and mom feel that way. Do you mind if I pray about it?"

And as she prayed God's love began to once again fill their home.

> Don't worry about anything; instead, pray about everything; tell God your needs and don't forget to thank him for his answers.
>
> Phil. 4:6 LB

Lord, thank you that I can tell you about our needs as a family. Help us to love one another.

Stored for Safekeeping

"Ahhhhh—" Cheri kicked off her shoes and lay back in the soft grass on a bank high above the river. Overhead the red-orange leaves of an old oak waved hello in the breeze. Beyond that the clouds shaped and reshaped against an autumn sky.

She wanted to save this moment—making time stand still. Holding it against the days when the howling winds of winter would keep her from coming to this spot.

Sitting up, she rested on her elbows, leaning slightly forward to watch golden elm leaves far below blow into the water—dipping, bobbing, curtseying to the swirling current.

"Thanks, God," Cheri whispered as she watched the leaves floating like tiny canoes to some far-off land. "Thanks for this memory."

What other memories has God given me? she asked herself. *What ideas have I stored in my mind? Ideas no one can take away?*

And there, watching the golden leaves drift downstream, she began to name them to herself.

Love, she thought. Love I don't deserve. Yet love which is given to me anyway. Love from God, love from my family.

And loyalty. Mom and dad sticking by me even when I do something wrong—forgiving me the way God does.

Freedom. Freedom to think. To be myself. A free spirit. Yet free to be responsible to others. A freedom I must never take for granted.

Fun. The good times. Seated on a log surrounded by darkness but within the flickering circle of a campfire. Stories. Singing. Laughter.

Warm sand. Warm sand beneath my feet as I raced for a lake. Flipping onto my back, floating in sunlit water.

And the winter wind biting my cheeks out on the slopes. New powder. Snow swirling upward past my turning, twisting skis.

The snap of a ball into my hands. Cheers filling the gym.

Yes, fun. Memories I have stored in my mind.

And knowledge? Yes, some of it hard-earned. But there when I need it.

And what else, Lord?

The tear on my mother's cheek, quickly

wiped away when I brought her a breakfast tray on Mother's Day.

The good feeling I had when I cleaned everything out from under my bed without anyone saying I must.

That unexpected smile from the boy that I like.

The time I found a baby squirrel lost in a window-well—and quieted its whimpers with an eyedropper filled with milk. The way it hitchhiked in the hood of my sweatshirt until old enough to scamper off on its own.

Yes, God. Thanks for those memories. And what else have I stored in my mind?

The hard times. When I was sick or someone I loved was sick. When I was scared, so scared, God. Or unhappy, miserable, in fact.

But what was there about those times?

Can I say thank you for those too?

Now, as they begin to fade, what is my memory of them?

Oh, I know, thought Cheri. You were with me then too. And that's what is stored in my mind now. That I can trust you, no matter what happens, good or bad.

But what about the future? What about the ice of winter when I can no longer see the leaves swirling downstream, reminding me of my thank yous?

I will grow older and everything will change. What have I stored in my mind for then?

Lord, do I know so much about you that no one can take it away from me? Do I know so much about you that I can expect great things even when I can't see them yet?

Yes, yes! That's it!

The elm leaves of yesterday float downstream, but above me the oak leaves hang on, a promise of color through winter until the buds of spring replace them—

Thank you. Thank you, Lord.

It's there now. A promise stored in my mind. Where no one can take it from me.

I'm ready to leave my hilltop.

Thank you, Lord. Thank you.

> Now glory be to God who by his mighty power at work within us is able to do far more than we would ever dare to ask or even dream of—infinitely beyond our highest prayers, desires, thoughts, or hopes.
>
> Eph. 3:20 LB

Thank you, Lord, for the yesterdays and the todays. Thank you even more for all that you are going to do in my life.

Pieces of Tomorrow

Do you ever dream about being the most popular girl in school? Or someone so successful that the whole world knows about you?

At one time or another most of us think it would be fun to be a woman who accomplishes something big. But let me tell you what happened to a friend of mine whom I'll call Luann.

One summer while Luann was attending writers' meetings she met an author much better known than she herself was. At the time her first book was selling well. Her second one had just been published.

The older author read her books and said, "Luann, you have a good deal of ability. I've known great writers and you will be one of them."

"That's just the encouragement I need," thought Luann. As she returned home, the tires of her car hummed a song of excitement.

But within a few days she tried to write again. The flow of words which she normally produced had slowed to a trickle. On her typewriter she could just as well have hung a sign saying, OUT OF ORDER.

She sat back and began to think. *What's wrong here?* she asked herself. *That encouragement made me forget all the times editors sent my stories back. I thought it would make up for my years of hard work. But here I am. Because I want to be a great writer, I can't write a word.*

It took awhile before Luann's typewriter raced along with its old ease. And the words came back only after she began wondering, "What is success?"

She thought about it for awhile. Is it wealth? Or fame?

No, it's not either of those things, she decided.

She printed some words on a large piece of paper and propped it up on her desk: "Success is doing well whatever job is right in front of me."

Someone else, an eleventh grade student named Lyn Crosby, put it this way:

The pieces of the puzzle that make up my today
Are pieces of tomorrow as well as yesterday.

As we work on jigsaw puzzles, we put together first one small area, then another. Gradually we fit those sections together until finally we see the entire pattern take shape.

In the puzzle of our lives, we can not yet see the whole pattern. Yet what pieces of tomorrow are we holding in our lives today?

For Luann and for many of us, one of the pieces is the decision of what is really important to us. We ask ourselves, "What is my goal for the future?"

As we think about what we want to do, we can remember the words written below a round window in the Library of Congress: "Too low they build who build beneath the stars."

We can reach now for those stars. No matter what dream is part of our puzzle—whether it's being a homemaker, a doctor, a scientist, an airplane pilot, a teacher, a nurse, an animal trainer or a TV personality—it's possible as a girl to dream big.

We can show our creativity through building a home where love is present. Or we can prepare for one of the careers which would not even have occurred to our mothers but is open now to us. Perhaps we will want to combine both home and career.

Whatever we do, God wants to be a part of the puzzle of our lives. He wants to have a living, vital role, not only in our todays, but also in our tomorrows.

And so, a part of our reaching is to ask, "Is my dream one of the pieces in a selfish puzzle?"

Or we can pray, "God, I want to help others. I give my talents to you. Show me how to develop them in such a way that they honor you."

Maybe the dream that is a piece in your puzzle began when you were nine years old, as mine did. Or you may be like singer Jane Henley who worked toward putting her name in bright lights.

She told a TV audience, "Once I wanted fame for myself. But then Christ became important to me. It's what he does in my life that counts."

Jane had fitted the todays and the tomorrows together, for then she said, "Success is allowing God to use the ability he has given me."

Someone else summed it up by saying, "What you are is God's gift to you. What you become is your gift to God."

What are the pieces of your tomorrow?

"For I know the plans I have for you, says the Lord. They are plans for good and not for evil, to give you a future and a hope."

Jer. 29:11 LB

Lord, I want you to have the most important part in the puzzle of my tomorrows. Help me to use my abilities according to your plan for my life.